Little Me BIG Dreams Presents:
SKYSCRAPER DREAMS

Early exposure is the key to success
Glossary & discussion questions in the back

JEREMY YOUNG

Illustrated By Larry Beamon
Edited By: Stephanie T. Young, Venus Brady, and Lana Cromwell-Jones

Copyright © 2015 Jeremy Young
All rights reserved.

DEDICATION

This book is dedicated to my biggest critic. The person who does not allow me to settle for anything but the best, and expects nothing but the best from me. This is to the person that pushes me daily to achieve everything that God has planned for me. To my headache and my help mate, my confidant and prayer partner, my wife. This is the beginning of an era. Thank you for believing in me, God knows I always seek your approval. Cheers to the good life!

-Jeremy

One fall Saturday morning the birds were chirping, and the sun's light was shining through the bedroom curtains.

I could smell mom's breakfast cooking from my bedroom. I jumped out of bed, brushed my teeth, and darted down the stairs to see what was cooking on the stove. Mom cooked a big breakfast like she always did on Saturday mornings.

Every Saturday morning, Mom made her surprise french toast; some Saturdays, they were topped with caramel, and other Saturdays she topped them with either chocolate chips or strawberries.

On this special Saturday, when I finished my bacon, eggs, and milk out came a huge plate of caramel French toast topped with powdered sugar. My mouth watered from the smell when mom said, "Hurry up and finish up, today is the big day!" Last week Mom and Dad promised to take me to downtown Chicago to see the lake and ride the huge Ferris wheel at Navy Pier. I was so excited that it took me forever to fall asleep last night. I waited for this day for 8 years! My whole life, I had never been downtown before so today was going to be great!

After I ate breakfast, I went upstairs to change my clothes. I could hear Mom shouting, "Make sure you bring your scarf and jacket. It can get pretty cool by the lake."

I rushed to get dressed and flew downstairs. Dad came out and said, "Son you look very colorful today. Is that the cool style? And I believe your shoes are on the wrong feet." I looked down at my colorful outfit, my mismatched socks and my shoes on the wrong feet when my father said, "Son, you don't have to be anxious and rush. You can take your time. We will get there. Besides, you don't want to become a man that is always in a rush."

I marched back upstairs and took a long look in the mirror. I had to admit, I looked weird! This time, I took my time just as Dad had said.

I put on matching socks and double-checked that my shoes were on the right feet. I grabbed a jacket that actually went with my outfit and a matching scarf. I went back downstairs, Mom and Dad were already to go. We got in the car and put on our seat belts. Mom said, "Since this is your big day son, how about you pray for our safe travels?" So I prayed "God thank you for my parents and thank you for the pizza You will get me later on," I peeked my eyes open a bit to see if my parents were listening on this part, "and protect us as we travel AMEN! LETS GO!!"

We were driving forever! I looked out the window at the lake as I dozed off for what seemed to be a split second. "Wake up camper, we are downtown," Dad said. I stretched, wiped my eyes, and then stepped out of the car. "WOW!" I exclaimed. It was exactly how I imagined, but even better. The buildings were huge! I felt like an ant as I looked up. I asked, "Dad, how do they build a building this big? Did God make these buildings?" Dad laughed when he said, "No son, God didn't actually make these buildings." "But God is the only person that is big enough to make these huge buildings," I replied. "These tall buildings are called skyscrapers," said Dad. "A skyscraper? They're called skyscrapers?" I asked. "Yes," Dad answered, "And people just like you and I built these buildings.

The people that make them are called architects." "Arc-ha-…" I said, trying to pronounce that big word. "It is pronounced ahr-ki-tekt.

They are people that draw and form these big buildings you see," Mom said. "Wow, so a person like me made this building?" I asked. "Yes, and what are they called, son?" I stuck my chest out and said, "Archuuplex!" Dad laughed when Mom said, "Say it with me, ahr-ki-tekt."

So can I build skyscrapers one day?" I asked. Dad replied, "Of course! When you graduate from eighth grade, you'll go to high school, and then you will go to college. After that, you'll be ready to make your own skyscraper." I wasn't sure, but that sounded like a long time. "How long will that take?" I asked. He said, "Well you are eight years old now, let's see high school, then college, looks like around fourteen years son!" "Good grief!" I replied. "That's longer then the car ride here!" Dad replied, "Oh, much longer! But, what did we learn from the colorful clothes earlier?" "Oh, I don't want to be a man in a rush," I said. "Exactly! Just be patient and you can be whatever you put your mind to, as long as you work your butt off."

During our adventure, I got to visit the Willis Tower, the John Hancock Building, and my prayers were answered when we stopped for pizza and lemonade. Finally after pizza, the sun began to set over the lake, the clouds were gone, but the stars began to shine. We headed over to Navy Pier to ride the giant Ferris Wheel.

When we finally got on the cart, I could see all of the skyscrapers. It was great! The big buildings had bright lights on them, which looked like stars. It was so pretty that I asked my mom to take a picture, and she did. The Ferris wheel was our last stop before heading home. We got back to the car and began to drive. I could barely keep my eyes open because I was so tired.

When we got home that night, I still felt like I was on top of the clouds. I got into my pajamas and crawled into bed. "I can be an architect (ahr-ki-tekt). I can build skyscrapers. God, please show me how," I said before falling asleep.

The next morning, Mom woke me up to get ready for church. She surprised me when she pulled out the picture we took of the skyscrapers while riding the Ferris wheel. I hopped out of bed and taped that picture on my wall. On the top of it I wrote, "Skyscraper Dreams." My mom looked at what I wrote on the picture and turned to me and said, "Always dream skyscraper-sized dreams!" And kissed me on my forehead.

Glossary

Adventure - an exciting or unusual experience.

Architect - a person who designs buildings and in many cases also oversee the building process.

Anxious - someone who feels uneasy, eager or uncertain.

Chirping - a short high pitched sound made by certain insects and small birds.

College - an institution of higher learning.

Curtains - a piece of cloth that hangs across a window.

Ferris Wheel - an amusement park ride in a form of a wheel that revolves in a circle.

Graduate - to finish a course or study.

Imagine - forming a picture or event in you mind.

Mismatch - to put together people or things that don't belong together.

Skyscraper - a very tall building with many floors.

Surprise - something not expected.

Weird - strikingly odd or unusual.

Group Discussion Questions
Answers may vary

Can anyone tell me why are big buildings called "skyscrapers"?

So is your school building a skyscraper? Why or Why not?

What is an architect?

When you graduate from eighth grade can you get a job being an architect? Why?
Answer: In order to become an architect, you are expected to have a degree in architecture. After getting your college degree, you must complete an internship in order to get hands-on experience. Finally, in order to begin practicing as a licensed architect, you need to pass the Architect Registration Exam.

Why is it important to *Dream BIG*?
What is your *"Dream"*?

ACKNOWLEDGMENTS

Thank you to my brother, David E. Young, who is the biggest contributor to this project. I'm grateful that you believed in me enough to sow a major seed to start this life-changing mission on exposing the next generation of leaders. I'm grateful for Eghsosa (Precious), we met at a event, he approached me and said "I want to sow a seed into this project." At that moment I needed that encouragement to keep going. And to every donation that was giving to support this project—without your donations this project will not be. To my good friend, Marquis Elliston, thank you for always encouraging me to keep striving to be great. Thank you for yielding your friendship. Thanks to my family and friends that support me.

Love ya'll!

-Jeremy

Jeremy Young is the founder and visionary of the Young Innovators of Chicago; a young professional social group whose primary focus is to empower and mentor youth across the country by exposing them to people and places out of their personal network. He's also a motivational speaker, activist, and youth advocate. Emerging from humble beginnings, this south side Chicago native travels across the city and parts of the country offering life-shifting workshops to youth on a level they can understand. Jeremy Young has worked beside world renowned leaders such as the Reverend Jesse L. Jackson, Sr. (Rainbow Push Coalition). The Motivational Speaker has been invited to speak at Chicago Public Schools, both high schools and elementary schools alike. Along with major colleges and universities, and major/local radio stations across Chicago, Jeremy has spoken on topics such as violence solutions, The power of the young vote, and motivating excellence etc. Jeremy's experiences from living in under privileged communities, and going to under performing schools has helped him shape and structure his innovative way of thinking. *"Be not conformed to this world but be ye transformed by the renewing of your mind"* In a Christ-centered environment, he serves as a catalyst connecting youth with mentors in various professions. His passion for youth has caused him to take a stand with them against the challenges facing them.

If you would like to contact the author Jeremy Young you can do so via Email: skyscraperdreams.info@gmail.com

ISBN 978-0-692-76368-1

www.ingramcontent.com/pod-product-compliance
Lightning Source LLC
Chambersburg PA
CBHW041809040426
42449CB00001B/34